*Spring*

1. Topiary Holly Trees. 9. Tulips.—Eclipse. Ivory Glory. Sweet Harmony. Godoshnik. White Triumphator. Black Parrot. Oriental Splendor. Bond Street. Dovor. Queen of the Night. Queen of the Bartigons. Red Parrot. Bokhara. Aristocrat. Nephetos. J. F. Kennedy.

*Summer*

11. Candy Tuft. Geraniums. Pansies. Petunias. Marigolds. Zinnias. Daisies. Rudbeckia. Begonias. Chives. Sweet Marjoram. Rosemary. Thyme.

*Autumn*

12. Chrysanthemums. Joanette. Dollyette. Pumpkin Rajah. Yellow Supreme. Red Headliner. Folksinger Carnival. Huntsman.

*East Garden*

*Planting Layout of North Side.*

*South Side similar.*

1800

# THE WHITE HOUSE GARDENS

## A HISTORY AND PICTORIAL RECORD

PREFACE—Patricia Nixon

A GENERAL SURVEY—Frederick L. Kramer

CONCEPTS & DESIGN OF THE ROSE GARDEN—Mrs. Paul Mellon

INTRODUCTION TO THE COLOR PLATES—Lloyd Goodrich

COLOR PLATES—Harold Sterner

**GREAT AMERICAN EDITIONS LTD.: NEW YORK**

FIRST PRINTING

Library of Congress Catalog Card Number: 72-87184
ISBN 0-913826-04-9

Printed in the United States of America

*I wished I possessed despotic power . . . for by no other means can I preserve the noble forest trees that are still left growing in different parts of the city grounds. It seems to me akin to murder to cut down trees that have been the growth of the ages; yet I am powerless and cannot prevent the ruthless destruction that is going on. Such trees! To be cut up for fuel! Trees that would form such durable and magnificent ornaments around our capitol, covering, as they now do, the whole hill and adjacent grounds. Yet I cannot save them!*

—THOMAS JEFFERSON

# PREFACE

Since 1800 the grounds surrounding the White House have been enjoyed by our nation's First Families, enhanced by official events and nurtured by devoted horticulturists, acquiring a distinctive character and unique beauty that blend the past with the present and reflect our country's deep appreciation of nature. Over the years these gardens have captured the imagination and attention of both historians and naturalists, becoming the subject of numerous studies, sketches, engravings and articles.

With the publication of *The White House Gardens,* there is now available to all a comprehensive reference on the landscape that has evolved from a countryside terrain to a stately setting of flowers, shrubs and trees. This impressive volume is not only a chronicle of the transformation and a vital document, but it is also an artistic treasury, alive with visual interpretations of the floral varieties grown and decorative arrangements displayed at the Executive Mansion.

As you enjoy this fascinating edition with its richness of textual detail and pictorial reproductions, I invite you to share in the gifts of nature it portrays and to experience the historic traditions which are so much a part of the Presidential Residence and of our nation's heritage.

Patricia Nixon

# THE WHITE HOUSE GARDENS

## *A GENERAL SURVEY*

by Frederick L. Kramer

The White House Gardens have been as much a part of American History as The White House itself. Ever since 1800, the year of its first occupant, the continual changes made during the development of The White House and The Grounds have reflected the aesthetic tastes of the various Presidents and the First Ladies in residence.

The gardens flourished particularly with the dedicated participation of John Quincy Adams, but not again until Mrs. Theodore Roosevelt took an active interest in them. For the most part, the grounds of the White House were regarded by most of its occupants and the public as a park-like area with grass, trees, and some pretty flowers.

However, it was not until the Administration of President John F. Kennedy that a serious desire evolved to develop the grounds of The White House into professionally designed botanical arrangements.

The plan of the city of Washington as originally drawn by L'Enfant in the late eighteenth century envisioned a President's Park from H Street on the north to the Potomac River on the south, between 15th and 17th Streets. The high iron fence surrounding the White House grounds today contains an area of just 18 acres. In addition to this, the President's Park includes an outer boundary of 52 acres known as "grounds south of the Executive Mansion" including the Ellipse.

The White House was designed in 1792, as a Georgian country seat by the Irish Architect, James Hoban. Today, the manicured landscaping of these rolling acres is beautified by the presence of some 250 trees of more than 50 species planted throughout the years by the Presidents. (See plan of Commemorative Trees, Plate I). This elegance stands in stark contrast to the state of the grounds during the time of the first Adams Administration.

John Adams, the son of a New England farmer, was the first occupant of The White House, and he evidently helped to plan the first garden. Mrs. William Thornton, a Washingtonian, wrote in her diary entry of March 20, 1800:

> *"Fine clear moderate day. After breakfast we walked with Dr. T— to the grounds behind the President's House which he (the President) is going to have enclosed and laid out for a garden. . . . It is at present in great confusion having on it old brick kiln pits to contain water used by the brick makers, rubbish, etc., etc."*

Unfortunately, since the writer did not elaborate any further, the type of garden planned is not known.

WHITE HOUSE, 1799
*After a sketch by N. King (Collection: The National Archives)*

Another observer described the appearance of The White House in 1800,

> *"The half-finished White House stood in a naked field overlooking the Potomac."*

However, the President's wife, Abigail Adams, was not as critical: *"The President's House is in a beautiful situation in front of which is the Potomac with a view of Alexandria. The country round is romantic but a wild wilderness at present."*

The crude state of the gardens did not change much when Thomas Jefferson began his term in office. In 1804, Thomas Moore visited the United States, and wrote in his letters to his mother,

*"The President's house is encircled by a very rude pale through which a common rustic stile introduced visitors."*

In 1805, a gentleman named T. M. wrote to President Jefferson asking if the President had any objections to the removal of the stile at the west side of the fence, from its present position to one a little south, so as to avoid the danger of falling into holes left by the brickmakers.

Evidently there was little progress in improving this situation. A year later, in 1806, an English gentleman commented on the house and its environs:

*"Only part of it is furnished, the whole salary of the President will be inadequate to the expense of completing it in the style of suitable elegance.*

*"The grounds around it remain in its ancient rude state, so that in a dark night instead of finding your way to the house you may perchance fall into a pit or stumble over a heap of rubbish. The fence around the house is of the meanest sort, a common post and rail enclosure."*

Jefferson did attempt to rectify this status quo of neglect. In 1807 he demonstrated his interest by submitting to Benjamin H. Latrobe, the distinguished architect who was at the time assisting in the design of additions to the White House, some plans for additions to the east and west terrace pavilions. In 1808, Jefferson stated in a letter to Latrobe:

*". . . Let the other half of the walls be immediately begun to be raised one foot higher. (2) The capping to be put on as far as it is already prepared, no gate or lodge to be attempted till we see the state of our funds at the finishing of the wall so far.*

*"When this is done so far let us begin the stone steps, and when they are finished and money put by for the planting of the grounds we will consider how best to employ what may remain of capping and Gates. So that the order of this work is to be: (a) the wall, completed and raised. (b) the Steps (c) Planting (d) Gates and Porters lodges, doing one thing at a time, finishing, settling and paying off one article before starting another."*

Thomas Jefferson was responsible for planting trees along Pennsylvania Avenue. He also supervised the building of what are now called "The Jefferson Mounds," on the

*Illustration of Gateposts topped with Eagles, 1810, at the approach to The White House. The pavilions built by Latrobe for Jefferson appear on either side of the main house. (Courtesy, The National Archives)*

South Lawn. These rolling rises create a sense of privacy for those walking near the main building. Numerous native trees were also planted by Jefferson, which unfortunately do not survive in the gardens today.

It must be remembered that by the time Jefferson left office, the country was officially only about twenty-one years old. Indeed, there were many more urgent needs confronting the President than the grooming and maintenance of his house. Quite understandably, the financial debts of the Revolution and the great economic burdens of building a young country gave low priority to the budget for the gardens of the President's house.

Similarly, the War of 1812 pre-empted the thoughts of James Madison, although it is recorded that he employed the services of a horticulturalist who suggested that a variety of flowering trees and shrubs be planted around the house. But contemporary comments of the day describe the gardens as "lying in gullies."

*Engraving by Strickland "The Blackened Shell of The White House" (Courtesy, Library of Congress)*

After The White House was burned by the British in 1814, the Madisons moved into the well-known Octagon House, now the headquarters and property of the American Institute of Architects on the corner of New York Avenue and Eighteenth Street.

Not until Monroe's time was the restored White House ready to be occupied again. Much attention was devoted to furnishing the new Mansion and a good many of the beautiful purchases made in France by Monroe, such as plates, table ornaments, and clocks, are still in use.

*The Breeder's Gazette*, of December 18, 1913, mentions the new Mansion and its occupant:

> *"Something was done in his time to improve the surroundings, though naturally the interior had his chief consideration. By 1821, the President's Square, as the grounds were called, was ready to be sown with orchard grass and clover seed, and with the leveling and grading done in the time of the second Adams it began to assume a park-like appearance."*

John Quincy Adams, son of John Adams, took special pride in the cultivation of the plantings in the gardens. One observer said of him,

*Illustration by Bartlett, 1839, of his engraving showing Tiber Creek, in the foreground, and The White House in the rear. Constitution Avenue runs along its course today.*

> *"John Quincy Adams loved gardening, and gratified his taste in a White House garden every spring and summer morning, after he had taken his swim in the Potomac which then washed the foot of the ground."*

President Adam's curiosity nurtured a serious study of his surroundings. In June of 1827, he wrote this description:

> *"In this small garden of not less than two acres there are forest and fruit trees, shrubs, hedges, esculent vegetables, kitchen and medicinal herbs, hot house plants, flowers and weeds to the amount, I conjecture, of at least one thousand. The casual poppies . . . all in flower, the mustard and anthemes in full bloom, the altheas still coming up and the wild cherries apparently stationary . . . the catalpa trees in full bloom and beautiful blossom. . . ."*

He also reported finding a white oak in the eastern seedling bed, and several oaks, peaches, cherries, plums, apricots, and rows of apple trees planted in the western enclosure. *The Breeder's Gazette* observes:

> *"In May, 1828, he notes the coming up of the black walnuts and other nuts, eighty-two trees along the northern border; twenty-one chestnuts, thirty oaks, twenty-five black walnuts, and eight cork oaks. He reports that Foy, the gardener, planted several rows of white mulberry trees."*

Remarkably, the President himself planted twenty rows of shellbarks, pignuts, black walnuts and cork oak acorns in the nursery westward of the row of transplanted cherries.

No other President to date has taken such an active interest in gardening at The White House as John Quincy Adams. The American Elm that he was responsible for planting still stands in the Southeast section of the grounds. (Refer Plate I). An extensive tree nursery was developed during his tenure. On May 23, 1828, he discovered several black walnuts that had been planted on March 22, and several almond trees, the kernels of which had also been planted then. There were also ash and ash-leafed maples, planted the November before, and in June, he counted ninety-seven Spanish cork oaks.

*Magnolia Trees planted during Andrew Jackson Administration as memorial to President Jackson's wife Rachel (Courtesy, Kiplinger Washington Collection)*

Andrew Jackson planted the Southern Magnolia trees in memory of his wife Rachel, who had died just before his inauguration. (Refer Plate I). These famous trees were saplings brought from his historic Tennessee home, the Hermitage. They now spread between the south portico and the west garden.

*The President's House—Gleason's Pictorial Drawing Room Companion, ca. 1854*

Ornamental iron fences were installed in front of the north facade in 1833. They were removed in 1902.

As the attention of each administration's First Family began to focus with greater enthusiasm on the enhancement of its official residence, so too did the watchful eyes of the elected members of Congress. The many State occasions and social events taking place at The White House gave more and more visitors an opportunity to critically comment about the decor and general aesthetic atmosphere of "their President's house."

During the Van Buren Administration, a particular event caught the public eye. Congressman Ogle, of Pennsylvania, was evidently quite distressed at the large sums of money being appropriated by Congress for the upkeep and the furnishing of the President's house. On April 14, 1840, in the House of Representatives, Congressman Ogle spoke strongly against a bill that was introduced to appropriate the small sum of $3,665 for alterations, repairs, and superintendence of the White House grounds.

His speech was so strongly worded and rich with evocative language that it was published for hopefully popular reading by the Boston publishing firm of Weeks, Jordan & Company. In part, here is what Mr. Ogle had to say:

## SPEECH OF MR. OGLE,

OF PENNSYLVANIA

ON

### *THE REGAL SPLENDOR OF THE PRESIDENT'S PALACE*

Delivered in the House of Representatives, April 14, 1840.

*"The House being in Committee of the Whole bill making appropriations for the civil and diplomatic expenses of the Government for the year 1840, Mr. Ogle of Pennsylvania, moved to amend the bill by striking out the following clause: 'For alterations and repairs of the President's house and furniture, for purchasing trees, shrubs, and compost, and for superintendence of the grounds, three thousand six hundred and sixty-five dollars.'*

*"Mr. Ogle said: 'Mr. Chairman, I consider this a very important item in the bill—not as to the amount, but as to the principles involved in it. I doubt much the policy of this Government in granting the Chief magistrate emoluments or revenues of any kind, over and above the fixed salary paid to that officer out of the Treasury of the United States.*

*. . . But Mr. Chairman, I object to this appropriation on higher grounds. I resist the principles on which it is demanded, as anti-democratic—as running counter in its tendency to the plain, simple, and frugal notions of our republican People. And I put it to you, sir, and to the free citizens of this country, whose servant the President is, to say whether in addition to the large sum of ONE HUNDRED THOUSAND DOLLARS which he is entitled to receive for a single term of four years, they are disposed to maintain, for his private accommodation, A ROYAL ESTABLISHMENT at the cost of the nation? Will they no longer feel inclined to support their chief servant in a PALACE as splendid as that of the CAESARS, and as richly adorned as the proudest Asiatic mansion? Have the People chosen that servant to superintend the great and diversified interests of the nation, or will they consent that his time shall be occupied with the vanities, luxuries, and pleasures of life?' "*

Aware that his speech would most certainly arouse threats against his sense of propriety by those of his colleagues loyal to President Van Buren, Representative Ogle then went on to praise indirectly his Constitutional right of free speech:

*". . . I feel inclined, however, to examine these subjects with all 'decency and respect' for the 'high office' now filled by Martin Van Buren, and I trust with a proper disposition 'not to speak evil of the ruler of my people.'*

*"Although I have a peculiar 'disenchantment' to discuss on this floor topics which have an appearance of involving personal rather than political considerations, still I am constrained by a sense of duty to offer some remarks in relation to the incidental revenues—the annual profits and expenditures of the President of the United States—the magnificent splendor of his palace, and the pompous ceremonials that 'hold sway' at this republican court, and which are by many well-meaning people imagined to be equally indispensible 'to preserve the dignity' of a Democratic Chief magistrate as of the despot on a throne.*

*"But sir, I am not ignorant that, in pursuing the course which I have marked out, it will become necessary to tread upon grounds that in former ages of the world were deemed, and in all despotic Governments of the present time are still considered, 'too delicate and sacred to be profaned' by the tongue of a plain citizen or subject. Who does not remember that the good Queen*

*Elizabeth hesitated not to enjoin upon her Parliaments that it was improper 'to deal, to judge, or to meddle with her majesty's perogative royal'? And history fully informs us that all such impertinent intermeddlers were disposed of in the most summary manner.*

*. . . I will not assuredly, be restrained from the fullest exercise of the freedom of speech. . . .''*

And indeed Mr. Ogle did not restrain himself from speaking freely about what he considered to be the wasteful expenditures of The Congress in order to subsidize the President's House. He described with great detail the elaborate design of The White House:

*''Let me now, Mr. Chairman, turn your attention to the amendment under consideration. It proposes to strike from the bill the sum of $3,665, intended for alterations and repairs of the President's house, and for the purchase of furniture, trees, shrubs, and compost, and for superintendence of the President's grounds. The 'site' of the Presidential palace is perhaps not less conspicuous than the King's house in many of the royal capitals of Europe. It is situated at the intersection of four spacious avenues, which radiate from*

*this point as centre. The 'palace-pile' is one hundred and seventy feet front, and eighty-six deep, and stands about the center of a plot of ground containing about twenty acres the whole whereof is surrounded by firmly-built stone walls and lanceolated iron railing with imposing portal abutments and well-barred iron gates. The main entrance front faces north upon Lafayette Square, and the garden front to the south opens to an extensive view of the River Potomac."*

Then Congressman Ogle listed the financial sums spent to date on the building of the President's House:

*"Previous to its destruction by the British army, on the 24th of August, 1814, there had been expended in building the palace the sum of three hundred and thirty-three thousand two hundred and seven dollars; and since that period the further sum of three hundred and one thousand four hundred and ninety-six dollars and twenty-five cents, in rebuilding the interior, and in erecting the two splendid porticoes; making together the large amount of $634,703.25 laid out on the palace structure alone, to say nothing about the very liberal sums that have been expended from time to time on the furniture, on*

*alterations and repairs, on the garden, grounds, stone walls, iron fencing, and for the 'stalls' for the Royal stabled steeds."*

With great relish, Mr. Ogle delved into the matter of the Gardens. Special note should be taken of his verbose descriptions of the variety of species and plantings:

*"Great improvements have been made within a few years past in the PRESIDENT'S GARDEN. It is situated, as before remarked, on the south side of the palace and is believed to correspond in its general arrangements with the style and fashion of some of the most celebrated royal gardens in England."*

*Engraving—The White House—ca. 1840 (Courtesy, Library of Congress)*

This reference to the White House Gardens' resemblance to the Royal Gardens in England seems contrary to the critical observations of the day, which lamented the sorry state of the President's gardens. But nonetheless, the Congressman's speech continued:

> *"It has a choice collection of both native plants and exotics, many of the latter having been gathered from almost every clime. Ornamental trees and beautiful shrubs have been 'selected with great care,' from the most celebrated specimens, and now are growing luxuriantly. The orangery, though not as yet on a very extensive scale, is fast improving. Rich and charming shrubbery and parterres 'greet the eye' in every direction. Nor should I omit to mention that, in addition to the numerous families of the tulip, the lily, the pink, the rose, and many thousand other sweet flowers and shrubs, which all the lovers of beneficent Nature admire, the garden contains some exceedingly rare botanical and medicinal specimens: and, for the 'benefit of the infirm,' I will give both the 'polite' and the 'vulgar' names of a few of them:*
>
> *Gerardia Flavi*, False Fox Glove.
> *So indago Lanceolata*, Golden Maid.
> *Orontium Aquaticum*, Golden Club.

*Engraving—(Courtesy, Library of Congress)*

*Circaea Canadensis*, Enchanter's Nightshade.
*Dracocephalum Virginianum*, Dragon's Head.
*Saururus Cernuus*, Lizard's Tail.
*Prenanthes Serpentaria*, Lion's Foot.
*Ophioglossum Vulgatum*, Adder's Tongue.
*Mimulus Matus*, Monkey Flower.
*Clematis Ordorata*, Virgin's Bower.
*Viola Primulifolia,* Heart's-Ease.
*Impatiens Maculata,* Touch-me-not."

Attention was also given to the many fine vegetables that were grown for the First Family's table:

*"But, sir, besides those rare, and no doubt very valuable plants, &c., there are some other varieties that are cultivated pretty extensively in the President's garden, which address themselves for admiration more immediately to the palate than to the eye of the beholder—such as fine Neshanock potatoes, honest drumhead and early York cabbages, white and red sugar and pickle beets, marrowfat peas, carrots, parsnips, &c. &c., with the abundance of the fragaria Virginiana, or strawberry, the dewberry, raspberry, &c., &c. In short sir, the President's garden, in all its arrangements and beauties, its trees, shrubs, vines, plants, flowers, and esculents, is in perfect keeping with the sumptuous and magnificent palace."*

Mr. Ogle shed humorous light on the functions of the Public Gardener, and how his time, paid for by public funds, was being utilized:

*"I may add that we have been informed, by an official report communicated to Congress in December last, that, during the past season 'the public grounds at the Capitol and PRESIDENT'S MANSION have been faithfully attended to by the PUBLIC GARDENER AND THE HANDS UNDER HIM. The trees have been skillfully pruned and trained; many choice or-*

*namental trees and shrubs have been planted; and the plants, borders, and gravel walks have been kept in SUPERIOR ORDER.' The report might have also stated with perfect truth, that men had been hired by the Government and paid out of the public Treasury, to pick up the falling leaves and pluck up by the roots, xanthium and rumex acetosella, or according to vulgar 'lingo,' burdock and sheep sorrel."*

Mr. Ogle revealed that during his four terms in Congress so far, he had only been in the gardens twice, and that on both occasions he and his companion were compelled, upon reaching the western end of the garden, "to clamber over the stone wall, finding the gates locked."

He alluded to the fact that the gates were generally locked except to those who visited with special invitation, or in the company of the President. This exclusion, however, did not apply to members of Congress, who were allowed to stroll through the garden and adjacent grounds.

John Quincy Adams next came under scrutiny from Mr. Ogle, because of the seemingly high expenses incurred for improvements to the Garden during his administration:

*"Before the administration of J. Q. Adams, the appropriations for improving the President's grounds had been very trifling. During his term, however, two considerable sums were voted by Congress for that purpose. The first of these grants was five thousand dollars by the act of 25th of February 1825, for levelling, grading, and improving the President's square. The second grant was five thousand eight hundred and sixty-five dollars by the act of 22nd May 1826, for finishing the fences, graduating and improving the public grounds."*

*The White House ca. 1841 (Courtesy, National Archives)*

Representative Ogle did admit that prior to the J. Q. Adams Administration the grounds were in a rather simple state:

> *"Prior to the disbursement of these appropriations, the grounds presented a rude, uneven, and shapeless appearance; not a few of the pristine sandy knolls and hollows still remained. The fencing too, was quite imperfect; but, by the exercise of a commendable economy in the expenditure of the sums just mentioned, and by the application of the money in the most beneficial manner to accomplish the objects contemplated by the laws, the grounds of the President were brought into fine condition, the fences were put in excellent order, the 'high' hills were made plain, and the 'deep' valleys were made smooth, and the entire grounds by the close of Mr. Adams' Presidency wore a style and finish quite acceptable to the taste and judgement of our plain, republican farmers."*

At this point, the real attack began. Mr. Ogle brought forth statistical records showing the allegedly lavish expenditures for the White House Grounds since the Adams administration and including that of Martin Van Buren.

*". . . In the mean time, be good enough to turn to books of United States statutes, for the last eleven years, and you will there discover not less than ten several acts of Congress appropriating large sums of money to improve the President's grounds, &c. I will now present the Committee with a list of those laws:*

*Act of 3 March,* 1829.

| | |
|---|---|
| For work to be done on or about the President's house and enclosures | $ 6,361.86 |

*Act of 2d March,* 1831.

| | |
|---|---|
| For alterations and repairs of the President's house, | 500.00 |
| For painting the President's house, inside and out, | 3,482.00 |
| For planting trees and improving grounds, including gardener's salary | 4,000.00 |

*Act of 2d March,* 1833.

| | |
|---|---|
| For alterations and repairs of the President's house, | 500.00 |
| For planting trees and improving grounds, including the gardener's salary, | 4,660.00 |
| For pedestal, wall-coping, railing, and foot-wall, | 10,000.00 |
| For constructing reservoirs and fountains at President's house and public offices and enclosing and planting fountain square, | 6,723.00 |

*Act of 30th June,* 1834.

| | |
|---|---|
| For alterations and repairs at the President's house, flooring the terraces, and erecting stables, | 6,670.00 |

| | |
|---|---|
| For gardener's salary, and for laborers employed upon the grounds and walks at the President's house, and for planting, ........ | 2,850.00 |
| For paving foot-ways, at the north front of the President's house, and making a gravel carriage way, ........ | 13,744.00 |
| *Act of 31 March,* 1835. | |
| For alterations and repairs of the President's house, and for gardener's salary, and for keeping the grounds and walks in order, including the cost of trees and shrubs, ........ | 4,200.00 |
| *Act of 4th July,* 1836. | |
| For alterations and repairs of the President's house, for gardener's salary, and for keeping the grounds and walks in order, including the cost of trees and shrubs, ........ | 3,460.00 |
| For constructing dwarf wall and fence, between the Executive buildings and the President's house, ........ | 1,165.50 |
| *Act of 3d March,* 1837. | |
| For alterations and repairs of the President's house, and for superintendence of the grounds, ........ | 7,300.00 |
| For constructing a dwarf wall and fence, from the south-west corner of the President's house, ........ | 1,300.00 |
| *Act of 6th April,* 1838. | |
| For alterations and repairs of the President's house, and for superintendence of the grounds, ........ | 4,815.00 |
| *Act of 7th July,* 1838. | |
| For laborers, and horse and cart and driver, employed at the President's square, ........ | 2,015.00 |
| *Act of 3d March,* 1839. | |
| For alterations and repairs of the President's house, and furniture, and for superintendence of the grounds, ........ | 3,465.00 |

For completing the special repairs, heretofore proposed in the President's house, including a deficiency in a former appropriation, ........................................ 1,511.22

$88,722.58

Mr. Ogle then went on to lament:

*"Here we have, sir, the enormous amount of $88,722.58, squandered by these glorious retrenching reformers, in erecting stables, building dwarf walls and coping, constructing fountains, paving foot-ways, planting, transplanting, pruning, dressing horse-chestnuts, lindens, Norway spruce, and Balm of Gilead; hauling and depositing rich soil for top dressing flowerbeds and borders, training and irrigating honey-suckles, trumpet creepers, primroses, lady slippers and dandelions, cultivating sweet-scented grass, and preparing beautiful bouquets for the palace saloons.*

*"The President's grounds contain about twenty acres. Our pseudo reformers have, therefore, expended on what they are pleased to call 'improvements' an average of $4,436.10 per acre, or $8,065.68 per annum. . . . And yet they have the effrontery to demand an additional appropriation of $3,665, by the bill now under consideration."*

To heap additional mockery on Van Buren's requested appropriation, Congressman Ogle proceeded to "poetically" describe the intent and results of some of the recent "improvements":

*"You will remember that by the act of the 25th of February, 1825, the sum of $5,000 was appropriated for 'leveling,' grading &c., the President's square, and that the Administration of that day took measures to carry into effect the intention of Congress by digging down the knolls, and by filling up the hollows, and in this manner levelling or making plain and flat the surface of the ground. But after all, Mr. Chairman, 'variety is the very spice of life,' and so thought our reformers. The survey of smooth lawns and gently sloping meads covered with rich coats of white and red clover, and luxuriant grass, make no delightful impression on their eyes."*

Ogle delivered his final insult with great pomp and an appeal to the hearts of the common man, while jestfully insulting President Van Buren:

*"No, sir, mere meadows are too common to gratify the refined taste of an exquisite with 'sweet sandy whiskers.' He must have undulations, 'beautiful mounds, and other contrivances' to ravish his exalted and etheral soul.*

*Hence the reformers have constructed a number of cleversized hills, every pair of which it is said, was designed to resemble and assume the form of AN AMAZON'S BOSOM, with a miniature knoll or hillock on its apex, to denote the n--pple. Thousands of the People's dollars have been thrown away on these silly fancies, which are better adapted to please the sickly and vicious tastes of palace dandies, than to gratify the simple eye of plain, republican freemen.*"

Andrew Jackson fell under the criticism of Congressman Ogle for the expenditures of $6,670 attributed to him and provided for by Congress on June 30, 1834. Most of the monies it seems were spent on "ERECTING STABLES," since President Jackson was a known lover of horses.

Mr. Ogle's final criticisms are directed to an appropriation of $3,465 in March 1839 for "alterations and repairs of the President's House and furniture and for superintendence of the grounds." His speech states:

". . . *I will present two or three vouchers for money disbursed by him in pursuance of that law:*

"WASHINGTON, *June* 14, 1839.

*Major* Noland, *Bought of* Wm. Buist.

March 22d and 28th: To 4 dozen of large DAILY ROSES, at $1.50 each .. $72.00
June 7th: To 2 VERBENAS, 75 cents each: 1 PETUNIA, 75 cents, ........ 2.25

$74.25

June 15, 1839. Received payment in full.

WM. BUIST."

[*Endorsed.*] "Alterations and repairs of the President's House, &c., $74.25. Wm. Buist's receipt for SHRUBBERY, June 15, 1839. No. 3."

"*Commissioner of Public Buildings,* *To* P. CASEY, *Dr.*

To 24 loads of MANURE, delivered at the PRESIDENT'S GARDEN .... $15.00
May 7. Certified by John Ouesley.

May 11, 1839. Received payment.

P. CASEY."

[*Endorsed.*] "Alterations and repairs of the President's House, $15. P. Casey's receipt for manure, May 11, 1839. No. 22."

"*Commissioner of Public Buildings, To sundry persons on account of* MANURE.

To Wm. Fitzgerald, 49 loads, at 37½ cents, .......................... $18.37½
Thomas Grady, 95 loads, at " " .............................. 35.62½
James Lee, 2 loads, at " " .............................. .75
Wm. Brown, 43 loads, at " " .............................. 16.12½
Michael Dooley, brooms 4, at 50 cents .......................... 2.00

$72.87½

I certify the above account to be correct.

JAMES MAHER."

[*Endorsed.*] "Alterations and repairs of the President's House, &c., $72.87½. Sundries for compost, July 1, 1839. No. 6."

*"Here you will observe, Mr. Chairman, Congress made an appropriation for 'repairs' of the President's House, and the money has been applied to purchase manure to fertilize his potato and cabbage beds. Congress made an appropriation for superintendence of the grounds, and the money has been expended, not in overseeing the grounds but in the daily purchase of large roses, verbenas, and petunias."*

As though he was exonerating himself for any "misdemeanors" he may have committed in bringing forth all of his charges, Congressman Ogle heroically stated:

*"Self-respect forbids me to denounce in suitable terms, these petty acts of meanness, and palpable breaches of offical duty. Be assured, however, that the officer who is not faithful over small things, will not be faithful over greater things."*

At last, after describing the interior furnishings of Mr. Van Buren's palace with its "spacious courts, its gorgeous banqueting halls, its sumptuous drawing rooms, its glittering and dazzling saloons with all their magnificent and sumptuous array of gold and silver, crimson and orange, blue and violet, screens of Ionic columns, marble mantels, with Italian black and gold fronts, gilt eagle cornices, rich cut glass and gilt chandeliers, suspended by beautiful Grecian chains, gilt eagle-head candleabras, French bronze gilt lamps with crystal gloves, bronze and gilt French bracket lights, gilt framed mirrors of prodigious size, large Italian slab mantel glasses, French gilt bronze mantel time-pieces, mahogany gilt bronze-mounted and rose-wood piano fortes, gilt mounted bureaus, superb mahogany wardrobes, mahogany gilt bronze-mounted secretaries, damask, satin, and double silk window curtains with gilded eagles, stars, and ornamental rays, royal Wilton and imperial Brussels and Saxon carpets, &c.," Mr. Ogle concluded:

> *"Sir, I am unwilling to grant appropriation of $3,665 in the bill under consideration. If, sir, it is inexpedient in these hard times to appropriate the money of the People for opening and improving harbors, for erecting light-houses, for constructing roads and canals, for improving the navigation of rivers, or completing the Cumberland road, and for other objects of real utility, I think the times are too hard to apply the cash of the people 'for alterations and repairs' of the President's palace."*

Evidently, the speech of Congressman Ogle had a definite effect on the attitude of subsequent administrations regarding the spending of monies on the maintenance and improvements of the grounds, and on The White House in general. (It should be noted that today, the refurbishing and collecting of furniture and art for the President's House is achieved solely through private contributions. It is the responsibility of The White House Curator to oversee the selection of these acquisitions, and to assure the American people that the President's House does maintain a collection of the finest art and furnishing that the country has produced.)

*(Courtesy, Library of Congress)*

*Illustration—The White House and Public Grounds—Ballou's Pictorial Companion—March 17, 1855*

Not until some thirteen years after Van Buren's time was there renewed interest in the grounds. It was noted that when Franklin Pierce took up his residence in The White House, he found that the grounds had been much improved, mainly by the genius of Andrew Jackson Downing, the first great American landscape architect, who had been drowned in the Hudson the year previously, when the steamer Henry Clay was burned. Mr. Downing was the author of several books on his specialty; and the task of beautifying the surroundings of the President's house was entrusted to him and an assistant, Mr. Breckenridge. The latter notes in his diary of August 1, 1842, the neglect of the grounds:

> *"In fact, very little had been done since they had lost the fostering care of Mr. John Quincy Adams.*
>
> *"Maher is the gardener of the Capitol and the public grounds extending to those round the President's house, where Ouesley is only the kitchen gardener."*

In 1851, Downing developed a new design for the President's Park, which was part of the plan for the grounds between the Capitol and the White House. Downing emphasized the English romantic style, but preserved the simplicity of outline of the White House grounds as recorded herewith in his letter to the President.

To His Excellency
The President of the
United States.

## Explanatory Notes:

To accompany the plan for improving the Public Grounds at Washington.

My object in this Plan has been three-fold; 1st To form a national Park, which should be an ornament to the Capital of the United States: 2nd To give an example of the natural style of Landscape Gardening which may have an influence on the general taste of the Country: 3rd To form a collection of all the trees that will grow in the climate of Washington, and, by having these trees plainly labelled with their popular and scientific names, to form a public museum of living trees and shrubs where every person visiting Washington could become familiar with the habits and growth of all the hardy trees.

The Public Grounds now to be improved I have arranged so as to form six different and distinct scenes: viz: 1st

### The President's Park or Parade.–

This comprises the open Ground directly south of the the President's House – Adopting suggestions made me at Washington I propose to keep the large area of this ground open, as a place for parade or military reviews, as well as public festivities or celebrations. A circular carriage-drive, 40 feet wide, and nearly a mile long, shaded by an avenue of Elms, surrounds the Parade, while a series of foot-paths, 10 feet wide, winding through thickets of trees and shrubs, forms the boundary to this park, and would make an agreeable shaded promenade for pedestrians.–

I propose to take down the present small stone gates to the Presidents Grounds, and place at the end of Pennsylvania Avenue a large and handsome Archway of marble, which shall not only form the main entrance from the City to the whole of the proposed new Grounds, but shall also be one of the principal Architectural ornaments of the city; inside of this arch-way is a semicircle with three gates commanding three carriage roads,– Two of these lead into the Parade or President's Park, the third is a private carriage-drive into the Presidents' grounds; this gate should be protected by a Porter's lodge, and should only be open on reception days,

Presidents Arch
at the end of Penn.a Avenue.

*(Courtesy, National Archives)*

thus making the President's grounds on this side of the house quite private at all other times- I propose to have the exit of guests on reception days on this side of the house, the entrance, as now, on the other side. I have not shown on the plan several ideas that have occurred to me for increasing the beauty and seclusion of the President's grounds, because I would first wish to submit them for the approval of the President.

2nd Monument Park.

This comprises the fine plot of ground surrounding the Washington monument and bordered by the Potomac. To reach it from the President's Park, I propose to cross the canal by a wire suspension bridge, sufficiently strong for carriages, which would permit vessels of moderate size to pass under it, and would be an ornamental feature in the grounds. I propose to plant Monument Park wholly with American trees, of large growth, disposed in open groups, so as to alow of fine vistas of the Potomac river. -

(Courtesy, National Archives)

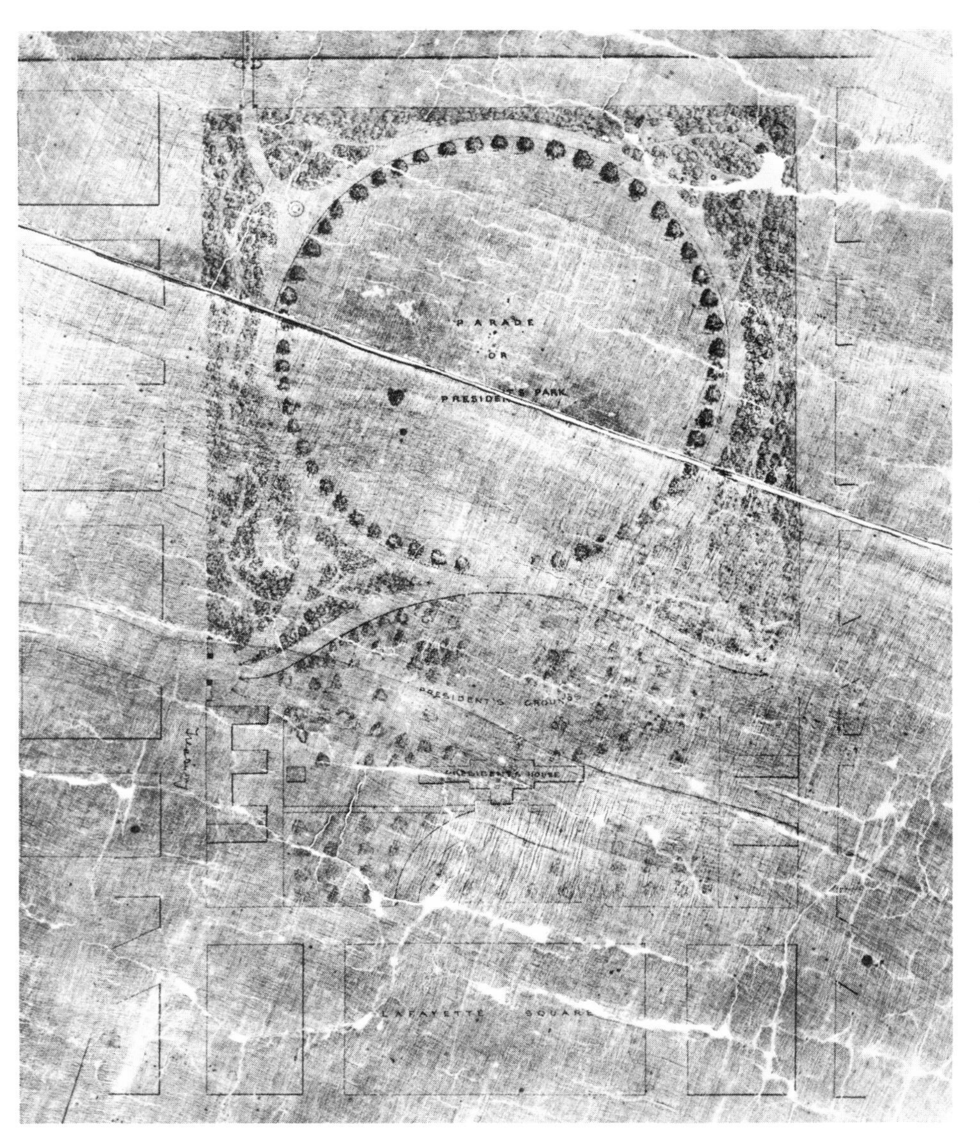


*Illustration of Downing's plan (Courtesy, White House Historical Association. Photograph Courtesy of National Geographic Society)*

*Engraving—Harper's Weekly, ca. 1858, Note: greenhouse on left.*

It was President Buchanan's niece and official hostess Harriet Lane who persuaded her uncle to have one of the big greenhouses built.

> *"A most fitting addition to The White House"* [commented *Leslie's* in 1858 on Buchanan's new conservatory.] *The President's niece Harriet Lane walked here among her camellias to escape the constant whirl of fashion. On public days visitors marveled at South American orange trees, aloes, and pitcher plants.*

*Frank Leslie's Illustrated Newspaper (Courtesy, White House Historical Association. Photograph Courtesy of National Geographic Society)*

With the arrival of the Civil War, the grounds of the White House suffered along with the rest of the country. The lawns were trampled upon by the thousands of troops stationed on the White House grounds and the many petitioners marching to make their protests known. Needless to say, President Lincoln saw little use in spending hard-pressed federal funds on beautifying the gardens.

The sad division of countrymen against countrymen at long last was ended in 1865. It seems that the people wanted to heal their wounds as quickly as possible, and all that would bloom with Spring began to appear with new hope and new life. The White House Gardens were no exception, as is revealed in this interesting account from *Harper's Weekly*, July 4, 1868, just three years after the devastations of the Civil War ended:

*MUSIC AT THE WHITE HOUSE*

*"One of the attractions of Washington during the summer—and the 'City of Magnificent Distances' has few attractive features during the heated term—is the Saturday afternoon promenade in the grounds of The White House to the music of the Marine Band of the Navy Yard. It is a repetition of the scene which is to be witnessed every pleasant Saturday afternoon on the Mall at Central Park, but on a diminished scale. In character the crowds are about*

*Illustration—Grounds of The White House, on a Saturday afternoon in June, Harper's Weekly, July 4, 1868 (Courtesy, The Picture Decorator Inc., New York)*

*the same; that at the White House is perhaps a little less democratic, and a few notabilities can be occasionally picked out of the crowd, which is of course largely made up of the Department clerks of both sexes.*

*"As our very beautiful engraving on the preceding page indicates, the Army and Navy are always represented; while as companions to the Chivalry of the service may be found Beauty gathered from all parts of the country. It has often been remarked by foreigners that there are few public promenades in the world where so many and such varied types of beauty belonging to the same race can be found as on the White House grounds. Representative beauties of all nations gather in the parks and on the great promenades of Paris and London and New York, and other capitals of the world; but at Washington, better than any other city of the country, one can see the various styles of the American beauty."*

The area immediately in front of the White House was a public thorough-fare. People were free to stroll casually under the porticos of the President's House, or to ride impressively by on their horses or in their carriages.

*Illustration from Harper's Weekly, March 17, 1877, showing people and their carriages promenading in front of The White House*

*Wood Engraving, 1869 (Courtesy, Library of Congress)*

Early in the morning President Grant's two sons, Jesse and Ulysses, Jr., were taken to school by two ponies, "Reb and Billy Button," as depicted in this sketch by Theodore Davis, which appeared in *Harper's Weekly* of April 17, 1869.

The custom of the Easter Monday egg-rolling contests on the White House Lawn was inaugurated by Mrs. Rutherford B. Hayes. Previously, ever since the times of Dolly

*Illustration—Frank Leslie's Illustrated Newspaper, April 23, 1877. "Easter Egg Rolling at Washington"*

Madison, this event had been held on the Capitol grounds. But since the lawns of the Capitol were apparently in ruin after each Easter egg roll, the contests were cancelled. After hearing of this predicament, the children were invited to the White House by Mrs. Hayes, where the egg-rolling contests have been held ever since.

However, even the White House lawns were damaged as noted in this account by the Head Gardener in April 1880.

Executive Mansion.

Washington. D. C. April 6th 1880.

Lieut. Col. Thos. L. Casey Commissioner of Public Buildings & Grounds

Sir:

I herewith submit to your attention a report of Damages done on Eastermonday March 28. 1880. in the Park south of the Executive Mansion. The two Police Officers & all the men I had on duty could not with all theire care prevent the large gathering of children &c. from doing harm to the grounds & shrubbery. Numbers of Evergreens are forever spoiled three of which had to be dug up. Paeonias arborea just in buds, were robbed of them

The flowering shrubs & low branching trees did not fare any better, allmost everyone is minus a branch or two.

The Grounds being wet, the Lawn suffered most, in some places the grass will never recover & will have to be replaced with new sod.

Some of the Brickgutters lineing the walks were damaged to some extent, Bricks taken up & scattered about. The most disorderly amongst the thausends on the grounds, were colored boys & girls from the age of 12. to 18. White boys atempted to make a Bass Ballground of the Lawns wherever they could & would do allmost anything but Egg rolling.

I am most respectfully your Obedient Servant Henry Pfister

Head Gardener

(Courtesy, National Archives)

This event is also suitably described in *Frank Leslie's Illustrated Newspaper* of April 23, 1887:

*"An egg-rolling festival, such as is celebrated by the children in many European towns, is annually observed at our own National Capital, on Easter Monday. It is great larks for the juvenile participants, as our picture plainly shows. To the adult spectators it is scarcely less amusing. This egg-rolling used to be done in the neighborhood of the Capitol; but since the time of President Hayes, the scene has been transferred to the White House grounds where there are plenty of grassy knolls.*

*"An unusually large crowd of people, old and young, to the number of several thousand, gathered here on Monday morning of last week, armed with baskets of eggs dyed all the colors of the rainbow. Children rich and poor, foreign and native, black and white, flocked to the festive scene, some accompanied by their nurses, others by their big brothers. Hundreds and hundreds of hard-boiled eggs were rolled down the slopes, and the children went tumbling after. They rushed, scrambled and rolled for the oval prizes, which when the shells broke under the rough usage, were eaten without more*

*ado. All this took place right under the windows of President Cleveland's office, and he enjoyed the spectacle very much, frequently pausing in his work to look upon it. Mrs. Cleveland was absent at Red Top, the President's country house, so she missed the fun. At one o'clock a great many of the children, with their nurses, flocked into the East Room of the White House to attend the President's public reception."*

By the turn of the century the grounds of The White House were extremely active with throngs of people coming from many distances to see and be seen at their President's House, particularly on those cherished Saturday afternoons when the Marine Band played on the South lawn.

But during the week, the pace slowed considerably, and the First Family were able to "take in" the gardens at their own leisurely pace.

In *Demerest's Family Magazine* of May 1890, it was noted that *"there was seldom any intrusion on the peace and quiet of the President's park, and seemingly, the severest duty of its guardian is to greet the pretty babies who, on bright days, came here for airing. In this, the lodge-keeper has cheerful assistance from his charges—the household pets, and Mrs. Harrison's collie, Dash.*

*Illustration—Wood Engraving (Courtesy, Library of Congress)*

*"Sunshine and warm weather usually lure a few loiterers to the graveled walks, but only gala occasions bring great crowds to the White House grounds."*

Mrs. Benjamin Harrison was a great lover of art and was very active in assisting with the ever-changing decor of The White House. She took great interest in the gardens, and even painted watercolors of the flowers. An example of one of her works is now in

*Watercolor by Carolina Scott Harrison. (Courtesy, The National Society of Daughters of the American Revolution)*

The White House Collection. Mrs. Harrison is said to have popularized orchids. She wore orchids to official meetings of cabinet wives during her husband's administration and at DAR functions (where she was the first President General of the National Society, Daughters of the American Revolution, when originated October 11, 1890.) As a result it became fashionable to wear orchids to important social functions in the Nation's Capital. It is reported that Mrs. Harrison was responsible for having orchids raised for the first time in the White House greenhouses. Through her interest, orchids were grown in much larger quantities throughout the country.

Under Mrs. Harrison's prodding, architect Fred D. Owen executed three designs about 1890. These marked the first concrete proposal to expand and enlarge the crowded White House. Included in the design were plans for an elaborate new greenhouse.

*Illustration of Harrison Administration's Expansion (Courtesy, Library of Congress)*

*Demerest's Family Magazine* of May, 1890, also revealed that the care of the gardens and conservatories was in the hands of an expert gardener with two or three assistants, while the presiding genius of the private grounds was the park watchman, whose neat lodge reared its gables modestly in the shadow of so much greatness.

This Victorian gatehouse is assumed to date from the 1870's and is shown here as drawn today by the contemporary artist David Hanna.

*Drawing of Victorian Gatehouse by David Hanna after photograph from Library of Congress*

*Engraving—The White House, 1891 (Courtesy, National Archives)*

Even through the administration of President William McKinley, the grounds of the White House were still open to the public, guarded by policemen only at the gates. By the time of the Theodore Roosevelt occupancy in 1901, the gardens were due for some changes once again.

The previously landscaped grounds had been laid out in the manner of the opulent mid-Victorian period. They were now changed into old-fashioned Colonial gardens by Mrs. Theodore Roosevelt, as is mentioned in this account from *The Christian Science Monitor*:

> *". . . It was Mrs. Theodore Roosevelt who helped her husband to change all The White House gardens. They put in old fashioned colonial gardens, one on the east side of the south portico and one on the west side of it.*
>
> *"Little walks were arranged all through the beds. Here old-fashioned perennials grew, such as phlox, delphinium, forget-me-nots, wall flowers, iris, English hardy daisies . . . and here and there a few roses. Mrs. Roosevelt liked them cut fresh and brought to her suite every morning."*

The greenhouses, which were on the grounds since President Buchanan, were removed, having fallen into irreparable disrepair. During the terms of President Chester Arthur, they had been much in use, as he had them filled with orchids and many varieties of roses. A report from Colonel Theo. A. Bingham, who was the officer in charge of the finances for the Grounds at the Executive Mansion at that time, illustrates how the

*Drawing by David Hanna after photograph from National Archives depicting greenhouses at turn of the century*

budget for the White House Gardens was used with definitely frugal concern. Perhaps Representative Ogle was still having an effect:

> *"The work required for the care of the grounds was performed during the year. This consists of mowing lawns, edging their margins, sodding or seeding bare places on them, cleaning gutters and drain traps, dressing gravel walks,*

*sweeping paved roads and walks, trimming trees and shrubs, caring for flower beds, etc. In November, 1901, the summer plants were removed from the flower beds and 66 beds planted with 64,600 early spring flowering bulbs and 5,000 spring flowering plants. In May the bulbs were removed and the beds replanted with summer flowering and foliage plants. A few trees and shrubs were planted. In the winter the lawns were dressed with manure compost, 413 cartloads having been used for the purpose, which was raked in the spring. Some unsightly trees were removed from the lawns, and the bare ground around the large trees on the sidewalk of Pennsylvania Avenue, in front of the grounds was sodded, and guards made of round iron, placed around them to prevent trespassing.*

*"In accordance with the usual custom, the grounds were thrown open to the children on Easter Monday, March 31, 1902. Temporary wire fencing was placed around flower beds, evergreens, small trees and shrubs, the large south fountain, and along the east and west terrace to protect them from injury. Considerable damage was done to the lawns, and the grounds were much littered. The cost of erecting wire fencing, cleaning up the grounds, and*

*repairing the lawns after this use was, for sod, soil, grass seed, stakes, and wire $71.50, and for labor $153.25, a total of $224.75."*

Mrs. Roosevelt's love for the White House Gardens is reflected in her official portrait by Theobald Chartran. It depicts her sitting on a white bench on the South lawn of the White House. (The portrait of Mrs. Grace Goodhue Coolidge by Howard Chandler Christy is also drawn on the grounds.)

An interesting and amusing correspondence took place in 1902 between Colonel Bingham and Henry Dreer Inc. of Philadelphia regarding the ordering of flowers and plants for the White House as documented by these letters from the National Archives. These letters illustrate the confusion which takes place over details and the lack of communication which results from the misunderstandings. Note also, that the last three letters change the date of the year by mistake.

Feby. 8th., 1902.

Henry A. Dreer, Inc.,
714 - Chestnut St.,
Philadelphia, Pa.

Gentlemen:

Please furnish the following described seeds, plants and shrubs for the White House Greenhouses and Grounds:

**Seeds**

|  |  |
|---|---|
| 2 trade pks. of Amaranthus brilliant, at 25 cts. | .50 |
| 2 " " " Antirrhinum Queen Victoria for | .25 |
| 1 oz. Aster Queen of Market, mixed, | .50 |
| 1/2 oz. " Triumph, | 1.25 |
| 1/2 " " Paeony fl., mixed, | .75 |
| 1/2 " " Comet best, mixed, | .65 |
| 1/2 " " Semplis branding, mixed, | .50 |
| 2 trade pks. Begonia hyb. fl. pl., at 25 cts., | .50 |
| 2 " " Erfordia or gracilis, at 25 cts., | .50 |
| 2 " " Dianthas nobilis, at 25 cts., | .50 |
| 2 " " " zonalis fringed, for | .25 |
| 2 " " Hmmemannia fumariae folia, at 15 cts., | .30 |
| 5 " " Primula abconixa fimb. carmine for | 1.00 |
| 2 " " Rubeckia bicolor sup. sem. pl. for | .25 |
| 2 " " Verbena Mammoth Aurora borealis for | .50 |
| 1 " " Ricinus zanz., mixed, | .40 |

**Plants.**

|  |  |
|---|---|
| 1 Aralia Kerchoriana, | 1.00 |
| 2 Geraniums silver leaved, "Mutt." at 50 cts., | 1.00 |
| 12 Phoenise rupicola, 2 inch pots, for | 1.00 |
| 12 Rose "Sunrise", 2 1/4" pots, for | .75 |
| 2 Primula New Giant hardy, at 25 cts., | .50 |
| 12 Livistonia Rotundifolia, 2 1/4 inch pots, for | 1.25 |
| 12 Microlepia hirta cristata, | .75 |
| 2 Gerleva Jamesonii, at 35 cts., | .70 |

**Water Lilies.**

|  |  |
|---|---|
| 1 Victoria Trickerii, trade plant, | 5.00 |
| 1 Nymphaea pulcherrima, | 1.50 |
| 1 " William Dougue, | 2.00 |

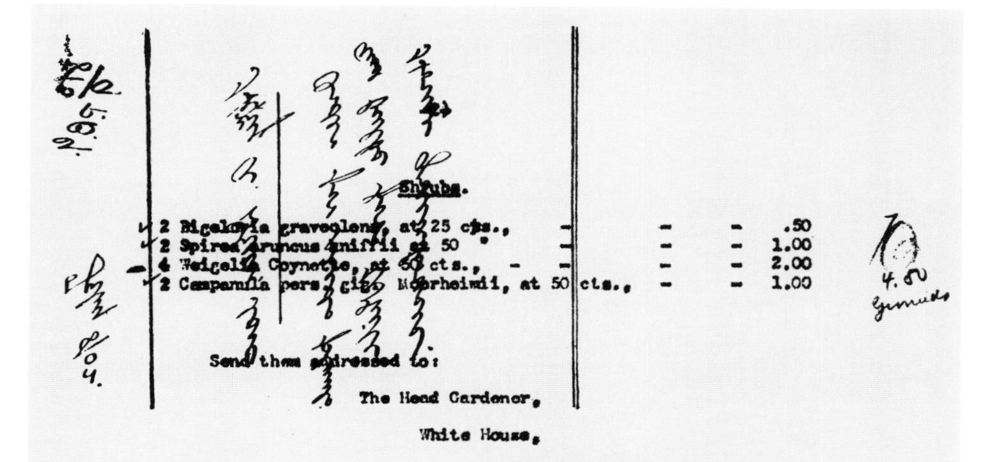

**Shrubs.**

|  |  |
|---|---|
| 2 Bigelovia graveolens, at 25 cts., | .50 |
| 2 Spirea Aruncus unifrii at 50 " | 1.00 |
| 4 Weigelia Coynetie, at 50 cts., | 2.00 |
| 2 Campanula pers. gig. Moerheimii, at 50 cts., | 1.00 |

Send them addressed to:

The Head Gardener,
White House,
Washington, D. C.,

with bill, accompanied by shipping receipt and this letter to this Office.

Very respectfully,

Theo. A. Bingham

Colonel, U. S. Army.

Pd bill $20.14 Feby 28/02
" " 3.00 Mar 22/02
" " 5.00 June 28/02

*(Courtesy, National Archives)*

Feby. 20th., 1902.

Henry A. Dreer, Inc.

714 Chestnut St. Philadelphia.

Gentlemen:

I return herewith my letter of Feby. 8th., ordering certain seeds, plants and shrubs, together with your bill for same.

You do not appear to have charged for the 1 packet of Ricinus zanz, mixed, at 40 cents.

Also, should not the one retail packet at $1.00 be 5 packets at $1.00, as ordered in my letter?

Also, you send 1 Aralia Veitchii instead of 1 Aralia Kerchoviana ordered in my letter, without explaining why the substitution was made.

Kindly return letter with bill and oblige.

Very respectfully,

Colonel, U. S. Army.

(2 inclosures)

813/9

FEB 24 Rec'd

Orders for growing crops accepted subject to crop failure, shortage or other causes beyond our control.

Perishable Goods when shipped otherwise than by Express travel at Purchaser's Risk.

All offers are made subject to being unsold.

Henry A. Dreer.

Established 1838. Incorporated 1892.

REGISTERED "DREER PHILADELPHIA" CABLE ADDRESS

Seed, Plant and Bulb Growers and Merchants.

714 Chestnut Street,

Telephone 13-76. Bell Bar 1618.

C.

Philadelphia February 22nd, 1902.

Col. Theodore A. Bingham,

Room 24, War Department,

Washington, D.C.

Dear Sir :-

Referring to the enclosed invoice and your favor of February 20th, would say we regret that in making a copy of your order from which to execute it, the copyist neglected to copy the variety of Aralia, consequently the wrong variety was sent. We will send the Aralia Kerchoviana to correct the error when we sent the 4 Weigelia Coquette, which are still due on the order. The 5 retail packets at $1.00 should be 5 for $1.00; "one" means 1 collection of 5 pkts.

Trusting this will make the matter satisfactory,

we remain,

Very truly yours,

Herbert G. Tull

*(Courtesy, National Archives)*

February 28th, 1902

Henry A. Dreer Inc.

714 Chestnut Street,

Philadelphia, Penn.

Gentlemen:

I send herewith for signature vouchers covering your bill of the 15th instant.

Replying to your letter of the 22nd in which you state that the Aralia Veitchii was sent by mistake instead of the Aralia Kerchoviana, you are informed that we will keep the Veitchii and have included it in the vouchers. The Kerchoviana you may send with the 5 Weigelia Coynette as suggested in your letter and you may include it in your bill for the latter. Please inform me when the Kerchoviana, the Coynette and the Victoria Trickeri needed to complete my order may be expected.

Very truly yours,

Theo. A. Bingham

Colonel .U.S.Army.

( 3 inclosures )

---

MAR 1 Rec'd

Orders for growing crops accepted subject to crop failure, shortage or other causes beyond our control.

Perishable Goods when shipped otherwise than by Express travel at Purchaser's Risk.

All offers are made subject to being unsold.

ESTAB. 1838. INCOR. 1892. PHILADELPHIA

**Henry A. Dreer.**

Established 1838. Incorporated 1892.

REGISTERED "DREER, PHILADELPHIA" CABLE ADDRESS

Seed, Plant and Bulb Growers and Merchants.

714 Chestnut Street,

Telephone 13-76.
P.O. Box 1618.

Philadelphia. Feb. 28, 1902.

Col. Theo. A. Bingham,

Washington, D. C.

Dear Sir:-

We are in receipt of your favor of Feb. 26th, for which accept thanks. We note what you say in reference to the Aralia Kerkowiana, and will make shipment of these along with the 6 Weigelias as soon as the ground opens enabling us to dig the Weigelias, which from present appearances we think will be within a very few days.

Regarding Victoria Trickeri, this plant will not be ready until early in May and will be shipped as soon as all danger of injury during transportation is over. It is a tender plant and it would not be policy to ship same until the weather is thoroughly settled.

Yours very truly,

Henry A. Dreer, Inc.,

J. D. E.

(Courtesy, National Archives)

March 28th., 1901.

MAR 28 1901

Henry A. Dreer, Inc.

714 - Chestnut St.

Philadelphia.

Gentlemen:

Referring to your bills of Feby. 26th. and March 5th. herewith, for plants furnished by you for the Greenhouses of the Executive Mansion, you are respectfully informed that:

1st. The Clematis "Countess of Onslow" has died. It was in bad condition when received.

2nd. Only one Clematis "Integrifolia" was received instead of the two charged.

3rd. The Clematis "K. Koster" was pinched off clear near the roots when received and will not grow.

Three plants as above should be sent us when you ship the four water lilies required to complete my order of Feby. 24th.

Very respectfully,

Theo. A. Bingham

Colonel, U. S. Army.

June 5, 1901.

H. A. Dreer Inc.

714 Chestnut Street,

Philadelphia, Penn.

Gentlemen:

Please inform me when we may expect to receive the three water lily plants and the one plant Victoria Trickerii required to complete my order of Feb. 14th (herewith) for the Greenhouses of the Executive Mansion, also the three "Clematis" plants mentioned in my letter to you of March 28th last.

Please return my letter of Feby. 14th with the bill for the four plants when rendered.

Very respectfully,

Theo. A. Bingham

Colonel, U. S. Army.

(1 inclosure)

(Courtesy, National Archives)

Orders for growing crops accepted subject to crop failure, shortage or other causes beyond our control.

Perishable Goods when shipped otherwise than by Express travel at Purchaser's Risk.

All offers are made subject to being unsold.

June 11

ESTAB. 1838. INCOR. 1892. PHILADELPHIA

Henry A. Dreer.

Established 1838. Incorporated 1892.

REGISTERED "DREER, PHILADELPHIA" CABLE ADDRESS

Seed, Plant and Bulb Growers and Merchants.

714 Chestnut Street,

Telephone 13-76.

P.O. Box 1618.

Philadelphia. June 10th, 1901.

Col. Theo. A. Bingham,

Washington, D. C.

Dear Sir :-

In reply to your valued favor of the 5th instant, we would say that the Water Lilies were shipped you on June 8th; find bill for same enclosed herewith.

In reference to the CClematis, we have refilled order for same. Enclosed find your letter and bills, as requested.

Very truly yours,

Henry A. Dreer, Inc.,

C. H. M.

(Courtesy, National Archives)

Sheep literally grazed on the White House lawn during World War I and President Wilson's occupancy. Their "cutting of the grass" released men for other war duties. Wool from the sheep was sold for the benefit of the Red Cross, and more than a hundred thousand dollars was raised.

The first Mrs. Woodrow Wilson planted roses in the Rose Garden in 1913 for the very first time. This garden adjoins the President's Office. Except for rearrangements resulting from the enlargement of the Executive Office in 1936, and from the renovation of the mansion in 1952, there were no significant changes made for almost fifty years, until 1962, when John F. Kennedy took office.

Having been impressed with the quality and care of the grounds of the official buildings he visited abroad on State occasions, President Kennedy invited Mrs. Paul Mellon to undertake the task of redesigning the two gardens. This transformation has been preserved with active interest during the succeeding Johnson and Nixon Administrations under the supervision and maintenance of Mr. I. Williams, the White House Gardener.

The design of the West Garden is a rectangle approximately 50 feet wide and almost 100 feet in length. It consists of a central lawn contained on the North and South sides by planting beds bordered by low hedges of holly and boxwood. The planting beds consist of various bushes, seasonal flowers and flowering crab apples which are viewed at intervals in each bed. (See Plate X).

The East Garden, now known as The First Lady's Garden, was officially declared The Jacqueline Kennedy Garden in 1965 by Mrs. Lyndon Johnson. During the nineteenth century this was primarily a lawn area with shrubs, flowering beds, and trees. The first plan for a garden is attributed to Mrs. Theodore Roosevelt, with additional changes having been made in 1913 and 1952.

Bounded on the north by the East Wing of the Mansion, the East Garden is also approximately 100 feet by 50 feet with a slightly smaller central lawn and like the West Garden contained on the North Side by planting beds arranged in a pattern with clipped American Hollies in alternate squares. (See Plate V).

These sections, as in the West Garden, are planted with flowers varying with the season and herbs which are used by the White House Chef. At the West End of the East Garden is a Pergola paved with old brick and at the other end of the garden is a small decorative pool. In the northwest and southwest corners of the garden are two large Magnolia soulangeana alexandrina.

In 1969, President and Mrs. Johnson created a small garden for the children of the President's House. This garden is located on the South Grounds adjacent to the tennis courts. It includes a goldfish pond and winesap apple trees.

Aside from the Lincoln Room in The White House, no other part of the Mansion is named for its former occupants except the Jacqueline F. Kennedy garden. This commemorative honor is truly fitting for this First Lady who did so much to change the earlier attitude about the gardens, which had led one foreign visitor to comment, "This parsimony betrays every sentiment of pleasure that arises in the mind in viewing the residence of the President of a nation and is a disgrace to the country."

Today, The White House Gardens stand meticulously groomed and preserved. Their magnificent appearance is a source of pride to all who have had the opportunity to tour the White House, or perhaps attend a reception on the South Lawn, or in the East or West Garden. Inside the President's House, flowers are very important too, as fresh arrangements are made every day for all the rooms and various occasions under the artistic supervision of Mr. Rusty Young. (Refer Plates XXI-XXVI).

At long last, the White House Gardens are a fitting and inspiring tribute to all those leaders of the country who have served as the President of the United States.

# THE WHITE HOUSE GARDENS

## *CONCEPTS AND DESIGN OF THE ROSE GARDEN*

by Mrs. Paul Mellon

The Rose Garden as it exists today was planned by President Kennedy. Before this, it had seen many changes as rooms and offices were added to the West Wing of The White House.

When President Kennedy asked that I submit a design to him, very little existed—only the large trees known as the "Jackson magnolias" that stand near the south portico were of any significance. There were no trees within the area to the west between the main house and the President's office. The planting consisted of several rows of privet hedge, Tom Thumb roses, poverty-stricken grass, and a few benches.

After his return from a state visit to Europe, President Kennedy was overwhelmed by the lack of attention given to this space, important, he felt, in receiving foreign visitors and guests of his own country.

The short intervals between a serious meeting and a reception in the main house could provide an interlude common to men the world over—a garden. It also would give serenity close to his office and a place in which to honor national heroes and to receive visitors. Therefore, one needed a lawn for the gathering of at least a thousand people.

The President wanted flowers—color—and garden steps constructed outside his office where he "could stand slightly above the level of the lawn but below those receiving the honors." A wooden mockup of these steps was built and he supervised the proportions—achieving simplicity with working levels.

The four large magnolias (Soulangeana Alexandrina) were chosen to soften the height of the main house and tie the garden to it. Their form is beautiful both in summer and winter. The grey bark can become pink, blue, even yellow, as the light changes, and the branches are separated enough to allow sun to reach the flowers planted below.

Each of these trees has its own planting plan beneath. Plantation lilies (Hostas) with their strong, varigated foliage contrast with the delicate epimedium and the flowers of spring and summer. Hyacinths, snowdrops, primroses, and violets—(sedum Seiboldi) working with the hostas make another strong line and allow the earth to remain empty if need be, for the color of the earth and its flat dimension have a beauty not to be questioned. The same formula follows throughout the garden.

There is a large overall outline approximately 125 feet by 60 feet. This is formed by a hedge of Osmanthius Aquifolium, a dark grey-green plant, hardy in Washington. It withstands the hot and cold days of winter without burning and creates a rounded, slow-growing barrier.

The ancient dark magnolias to the east are softened by hawthorns, crabapples, and holly, with spring bulbs planted beneath. There is a small stone path—that belonged to the children—winding through this and hidden by the informal terrace facing the garden.

The larger bushes of English box (Buxus Semper Virens) are traditional in this type of planting and to most southern gardens.

The influence of both Washington and Jefferson, as well as Monroe, are manifest in the choice of trees and shrubs throughout the garden, for President Kennedy shared, as they did, gardens as a part of life.

The roses are mostly pale colors and white (and now include the John F. Kennedy rose), the reason being that too many red roses mixed with other flowers tend to give a garden a heaviness and sadness that do not belong. Red roses are often the most beautiful of all roses, but they are better planted together, or with flowers related to them. Here we planted them with large red cabbages, blue thistles, and heliotrope.

When winter comes and the garden is turned under, the roses and perennials remain in the ground along with 2000 tulip bulbs and 8000 grape hyacinths planted for spring. The grape hyacinths make two long ribbon borders of deep lapis blue in late April.

The bright red berries stay a long time on the crabapples, hawthorns, and hollies. The outlines of the four magnolias catch the snow and cast shadows in the cold winter atmosphere that make the garden alive and strong during this time of year.

The lawn is planted with Merion Blue grass and fescue. Before planting anything, this space had to be excavated four feet in the ground, where we found rubble belonging to each change in The White House, as well as horseshoes dating back to the Civil War. It was here—years ago—that Abigail Adams hung out her wash.

President Kennedy took endless interest in building this garden, and with his interest grew the enthusiasm of those who worked on it to perfect every detail. It was built under the Department of the Interior and Mr. Whitey Williams, who was working at the Maryland Aquatic Gardens. He left there and came as superintendent to The White House Gardens and has remained ever since. Both he and I were aided by the knowledge and loyalty of Perry Wheeler, a well-known landscape gardener who lives in Washington. His never-ending quiet presence and experience had a great deal to do with the perfection of this garden. Finally, and providing a liaison between the gardens outside and flower decors inside The White House were Mr. J. B. West (Head Usher) and Mr. Rusty Young in charge of the Flower Room.

# THE WHITE HOUSE GARDENS

## *INTRODUCTION TO THE COLOUR PLATES*

by Lloyd Goodrich

In this day of omnipresent color photography we are apt to forget that before the invention of the camera, pictures of any kind were made by artists. Artists were not only the visual historians and storytellers of society, they also carried on all the manifold utilitarian functions of picture-making. To describe a thing visually—a much more direct way than to describe it verbally—one made a drawing of it. But within the last hundred years this essential function of the artist has been largely taken over by the camera.

And yet the camera is far from being the most satisfactory means of representation. The camera has only one eye, whereas the artist has two, so that he can see a little around the edges of an object and realize its three-dimensional form and substance; and his hand can render these qualities more completely than the camera can. And the artist's eye and hand are governed by a mind that subordinates surface appearances, and concentrates on the thing-in-itself. Hence the best ornithological books are illustrated by artists, not by the camera, and even the *Scientific American* often uses drawings in preference to photographs.

Of all the historic fields of pictorial recording, that of flowers and plants and trees has always been one of the most important, and one of the most pleasurable. There is an affinity between flowers and art, for flowers are themselves works of art, products of centuries of human cultivation, and of mankind's search for perfection in form and color. Botanical representation has a long history, from the Egyptians, Greeks and Romans through the medieval illuminators of manuscripts, the seventeenth-century Dutch and Flemish still-life painters, Redouté and his enchanting record of the roses at Malmaison, and Audubon with the profusion of foliage, blossoms and fruit amid which he placed his birds. The achievements of such artists prove that in the hands of gifted individuals, botanical records can also be pure works of art; and that there is no necessary conflict between scientific accuracy and aesthetic values.

This age-old pictorial tradition is continued in our day by Harold Sterner's documentary watercolors and drawings. Sterner has unusual qualifications for this form of art. He was born and brought up in the world of art; his father Albert Sterner was an accomplished portraitist and illustrator, and his mother Marie Sterner was a discriminating gallery director. He had no need of art schools, since art was the central fact of his childhood and youth. At thirteen he was already a professional, painting watercolor views of the gardens of Newport. When it came time to decide on a career, he chose architecture; but through the years he has continued to paint and draw, so that he can be said to lead a double creative life. His paintings with their highly personal combination of fantastic imagery, evocative poetry and technical skill have earned him a special place in contemporary art.

Gifted with a broad range of interests, Sterner is an indefatigable worker whose mind and hands are never idle. Parallel with his paintings he has produced several series of documentary drawings and watercolors covering a wide variety of objects, natural and man-made. His renderings of historic American buildings and his portraits of nineteenth-century sailing craft and steamships are at once impeccably accurate and beautiful in their craftsmanship. He has made a complete graphic record of his own home on Long Island. The house and its furniture, silverware and china; the garden with its flora, and even its fauna of butterflies and insects—a visual inventory marked by loving care in representing these objects of nature and man. The culmination of his achievements in this field is the present volume on the gardens and grounds of the White House. In this delightful pictorial record Harold Sterner demonstrates that, today as in the past, science and art can be happily wedded.

Lloyd Goodrich

# *COLOR PLATES BY HAROLD STERNER*


*I.* *Plan of Presidential Grounds.*
*II.* *Commemorative Trees.*
*III.* *Commemorative Trees.*
*IV.* *Flowering Trees.*
*V.* *Plan of East Garden.*
*VI.* *Spring Flowers • East and West Gardens.*
*VII.* *Spring Flowers • East and West Gardens.*
*VIII.* *Tulips • East and West Gardens.*
*IX.* *Tulips • East and West Gardens.*
*X.* *Herbs and Border Plants • East Garden.*
*XI.* *Plan of West Garden.*
*XII.* *Roses • West Garden.*
*XIII.* *Roses • West Garden.*
*XIV.* *Spring and Summer Flowers • East and West Gardens.*
*XV.* *Spring and Summer Flowers • East and West Gardens.*
*XVI.* *Spring and Summer Flowers • East and West Gardens.*
*XVII.* *Spring and Summer Flowers • East and West Gardens.*
*XVIII.* *Spring and Summer Flowers • East and West Gardens.*
*XIX.* *Summer Flowers • East and West Gardens.*
*XX.* *Autumn Flowers • East and West Gardens.*
*XXI.* *Kennedy Administration • Flower Arrangement.*
*XXII.* *Kennedy Administration • Flower Arrangement.*
*XXIII.* *Kennedy Administration • Flower Arrangement.*
*XXIV.* *Kennedy Administration • Flower Arrangement.*
*XXV.* *Johnson Administration • Flower Arrangement.*
*XXVI.* *Nixon Administration • Flower Arrangement.*

# *Plate I*

## *The White House Gardens and Commemorative Trees*

A. THE MOUNDS. Thomas Jefferson.
B. AMERICAN ELM. John Q. Adams.
C. MAGNOLIA GRANDIFLORA. Andrew Jackson.
D. SCARLET OAK. Benjamin Harrison.
E. JAPANESE MAPLES. Grover Cleveland.
F. AMERICAN ELM. Woodrow Wilson.
G. MAGNOLIA GRANDIFLORA. Warren G. Harding.
H. EUROPEAN WHITE BIRCH. Calvin Coolidge.
I. AMERICAN ELM. Herbert Hoover.
J. WHITE OAK. Herbert Hoover.
K. MAGNOLIA GRANDIFLORA. Franklin D. Roosevelt.
L. WHITE OAK. Franklin D. Roosevelt.
M. LITTLE LEAF LINDENS. Franklin D. Roosevelt.
N. AMERICAN BOXWOOD. Harry S. Truman.
O. WHITE OAK. Herbert Hoover.
P. PIN OAK. Dwight D. Eisenhower.
Q. RED OAK. Dwight D. Eisenhower.
R. NORTHERN RED OAK. Dwight D. Eisenhower.
S. THE ROSE GARDEN. John F. Kennedy.
T. MAGNOLIA SOULANGEANA. John F. Kennedy.
U. APPLE. John F. Kennedy.
V. THE EAST GARDEN. Jacqueline Kennedy.
W. DARLINGTON OAK. Lyndon B. Johnson.
X. WILLOW OAK. Lyndon B. Johnson.
Y. FERN LEAF BEECH. Mrs. Richard Nixon.
Z. SEQUOIA. Mrs. Richard Nixon.
Bb. BEECH. Mrs. Lyndon Johnson.
Tc. TENNIS COURT.
Cg. CHILDREN'S GARDEN. Lyndon B. Johnson.
Fo. FOUNTAIN.

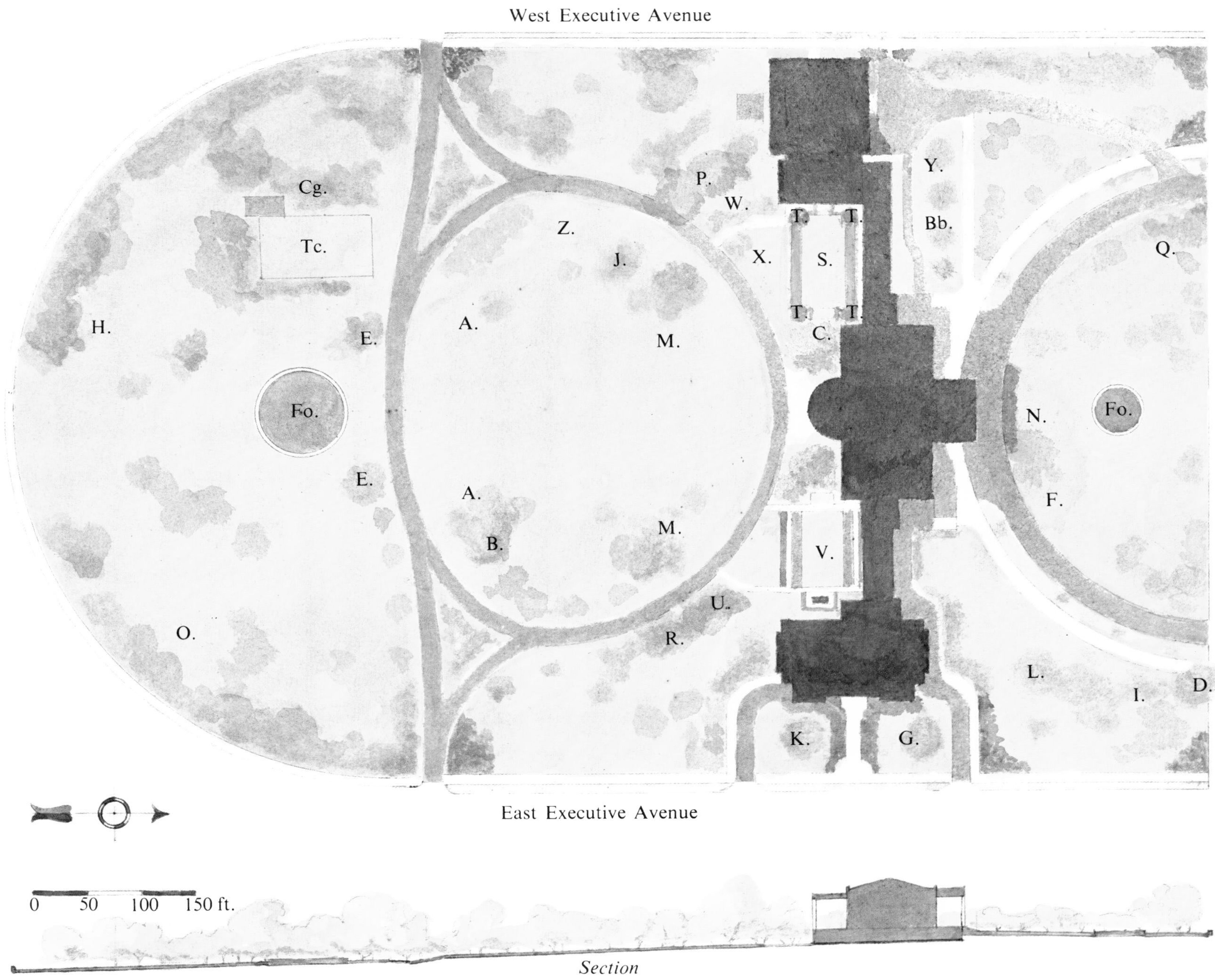
West Executive Avenue
East Executive Avenue
Pennsylvania Avenue
Cg.
Tc.
H.
E.
Fo.
E.
O.
A.
A.
B.
Z.
J.
M.
M.
P.
W.
X.
U.
R.
T.
T.
S.
T.
T.
C.
V.
Y.
Bb.
Q.
N.
Fo.
F.
L.
I.
D.
K.
G.
0
50
100
150 ft.

*Section*

# *Plate II*

## *Commemorative Trees*

A. Black Walnut. *Jugens nigra.*
B. Magnolia. *Magnolia grandiflora.*
C. European Birch. *Betula.*
D. American Elm. *Ulmus americana.*

A.
B.
C.
D.

# *Plate III*

## *Commemorative Trees*

A. Red Oak. *Quercus borealis.*
B. Scarlet Oak. *Quercus caccinea.*
C. White Oak. *Quercus garryanna.*
D. Willow Oak. *Quercus phellos.*

A.
B.
C.
D.

# *Plate IV*

## *Flowering Trees*

A. Katherine Crab Apple. *Malus katherine.*
B. Flowering Dogwood. *Cornus florida.*
C. Magnolia. *Magnolia soulangeana.*
D. Great Laurel. *Rhododendron maximum.*

A.
B.
C.
D.

# *Plate V*

## *Plan of East Garden*

1. Topiary Holly Trees.
2. Lawn.
3. Holly. *Crenata convexa.*
4. Osmanthus. *Osmanthus ilicifolius.*
5. Kingsville Boxwood. *Buxus Microphylla compacta.*
6. Small English Boxwood. *Buxus sempervirens.*

A. Pergola.
B. Planting Beds.
M. Magnolia. *Magnolia soulangeana.*
P. Pool.
S. Seats.

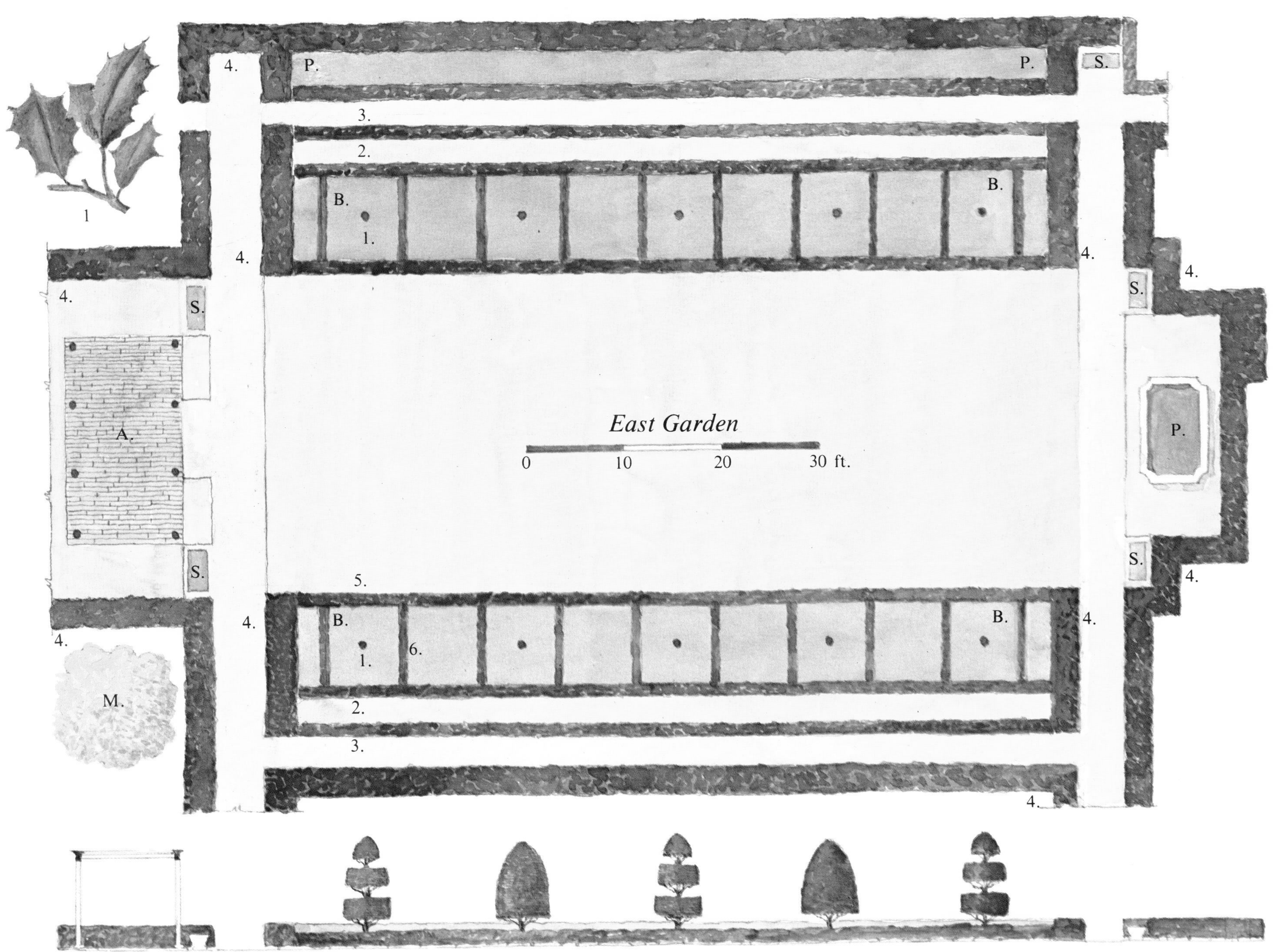
4.
P.
P.
S.
3.
2.
B.
B.
1.
1
4.
4.
4.
4.
S.
A.
East Garden
0
10
20
30 ft.
P.
S.
S.
5.
4.
4.
B.
B.
4.
4.
1.
6.
M.
2.
3.
4.
Section

# *Plate VI*

## *Spring Flowers • East and West Gardens*

A. Chinodoxa. *Chinodoxa.* a Bulb.
B. Squill. *Scilla sibirica.*
C. Fritillaria. *Fritillaria imperialis.* c Bulb.
D. Grape Hyacinth. *Muscari botryoides.* d Bulb.

A.
a.
B.
C.
c.
D.
d.

# *Plate VII*

## *Spring Flowers • East and West Gardens*

A. "Cheerfulness." *Narcissus hybrid.* a. Bulb.
B. "Shot Silk." *Narcissus miniature.*
C. "Yellow Cheerfulness." *Narcissus hybrid.*
D. Jonquil. *Narcissus jonquilla.*
E. Large Cupped Daffodil. *Narcissus hybrid.* e. Detail.
$F^1$ and $F^2$ Large Dutch Crocus "Violet Queen." "Cream Beauty." *Crocus.* f. Bulb.

B.
e.
E.
a.
f.
A.
C.
D.
F¹.-F².

# *Plate VIII*

## *Tulips • East and West Garden*

A. Darwin Tulip "Queen of the Bartigons." *Tulipa.* a. Detail. a[1]. Bulb.
B. Darwin Tulip "Queen of the Night." *Tulipa.* b. Detail. b[1]. Bulb.
C. Darwin Tulip "Sweet Harmony." *Tulipa.*

a.
b.
A.
a1.
B.
b1.
C.

# *Plate IX*

## *Tulips • East and West Garden*

A. Darwin Tulip "Eclipse." *Tulipa.*
B. Lily Flowered Tulip "Queen of Sheba." *Tulipa.* b. Bulb.
C. Lily Flowered Tulip "Triumphator." *Tulipa.* c. Detail.
D. Darwin Hybrid Tulip "Godoshnik." *Tulipa.*

A.
B.
c.
C.
D.

## *Plate X*

### *Herbs and Border Plants • East Garden*

A. Marjoram. *Majorana hortensis.*
B. Thyme. *Thymus vulgaris.*
C. Rosemary. *Rosmarinus officinalis.*
D. Chives. *Allium schoenoprasum.*
E. Basil. *Ocimum basilicum.*
F. Catmint. *Nepeta fassenii.*
G. Dusty Miller. *Senecio cineraria.*
H. Lady's Mantle. *Alchemilla vulgaris.*

A.
B.
C.
D.
E.
F.
G.
H.

# *Plate XI*

## *Plan of West Garden*

1. Katherine Crab Apple. *Malus katherine.*
2. Rose Bushes. *Rosacea.*
3. Dusty Miller. *Santolina.*
4. Holly. *Osmanthus ilicifolius.*
5. Pillow Boxwood. *Buxus microphylla.*
6. Small English Boxwood.
7. English Boxwood. *Buxus sempervirens.*

B. Planting Beds.
F. Flagstone Terrace
M. Magnolia. *Magnolia soulangeana.*
S. Flagstone Steps.

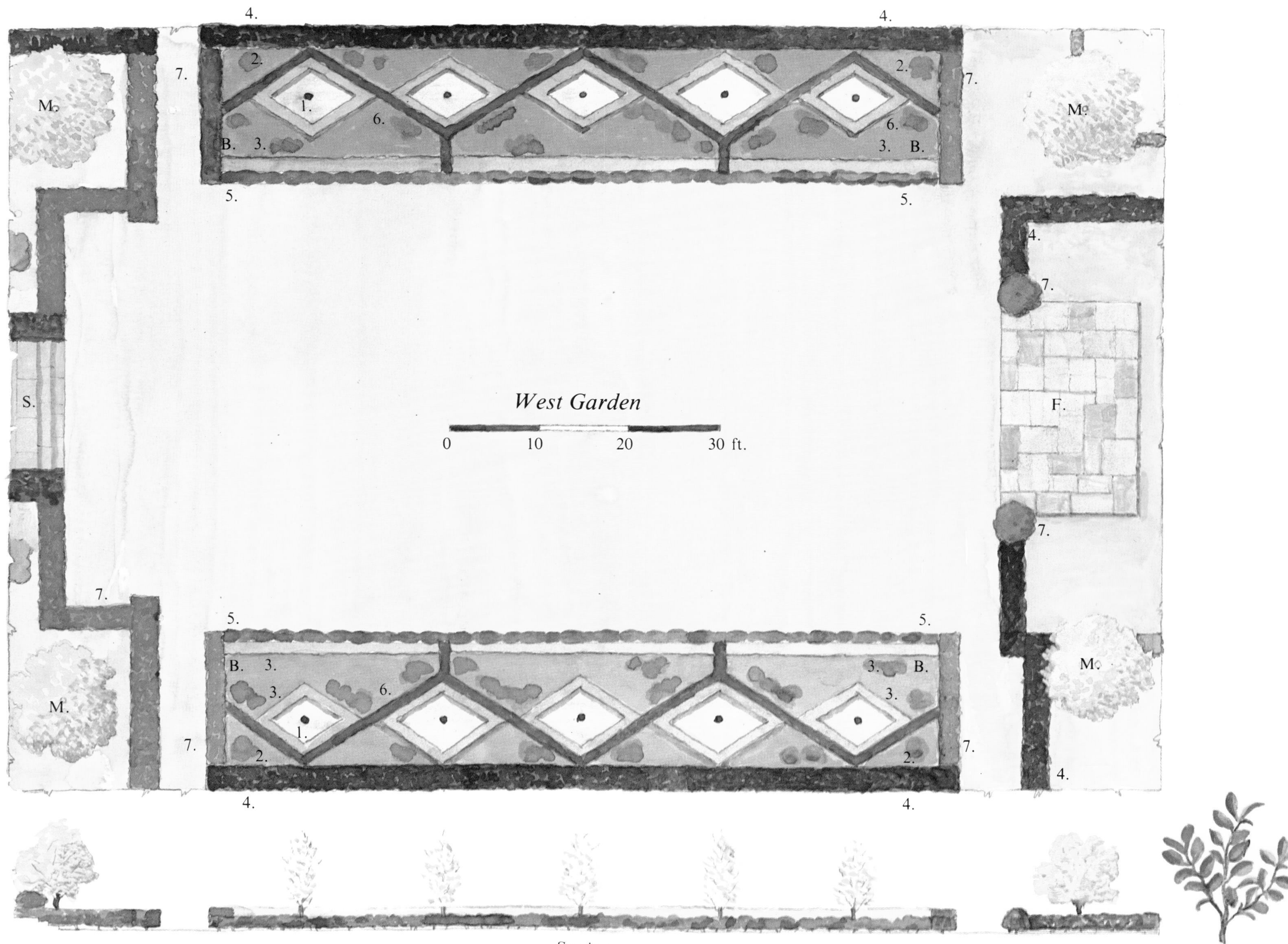
4.
4.
7.
2.
2.
7.
M.
1.
6.
6.
M.
B.
3.
3.
B.
5.
5.
4.
7.
S.
West Garden
0
10
20
30 ft.
F.
7.
7.
5.
5.
B.
3.
3.
B.
3.
6.
3.
M.
1.
M.
7.
2.
2.
7.
4.
4.
4.
Section

# *Plate XII*

## *Roses • West Garden*

A. Grandiflora Rose "Queen Elizabeth." *Rosacea.*
B. Hybrid Tea Rose "Pascali." *Rosacea.*

A.
B.

# *Plate XIII*

## *Roses • West Garden*

A. Hybrid Tea Rose "Kings Ransom." *Rosacea.*
B. Shrub Rose "Nevada." *Rosacea.*

A.
B.

# *Plate XIV*

## *Spring and Summer Flowers • East and West Gardens*

A. Peonies. *Paeonia officinalis.*
A[1]. Peony. *Paeonia lactiflora.*
B. Day Lily. *Hemerocallis fulva.*
C. Oriental Poppy. *Papaver orientale.* c. Detail.

A.
A1.
B.
C.
c.

# *Plate XV*

*Spring and Summer Flowers • East and West Gardens*

A. Petunias. *Petunia hybrid.*
B. Pansies. *Viola hybrid.*
C. Zinnias. *Zinnia haengena.*
C. Zinnias. *Zinnia elegans.*

A.
A.
C.
B.
B.
C.

# *Plate XVI*

## *Spring and Summer Flowers • East and West Gardens*

A. Michaelmas Daisy. *Aster frikartii.*
B. Black Eyed Susan. *Rudbeckia speciosa.*
C. Blanket Flower. *Gaillardia.*

A.
B.
C.

# *Plate XVII*

## *Spring and Summer Flowers • East and West Gardens*

A. Candy Tuft. *Iberis sempervirens.*
B. Japanese Anemone. *Anemone hybrida.*
C. c. Nicotiana. *Nicotiana elata.*

A.
B.
c.
C.

# *Plate XVIII*

## *Spring and Summer Flowers • East and West Gardens*

A. Delphinium. *Delphinium elatum.*
B. Heliotrope. *Heliotropum peruviana.*
C. Salvia. *Salvia pitcherii.*

A.
B.
C.

# *Plate XIX*

## *Summer Flowers • East and West Gardens*

A. Marigold "Rusty Red." *Tagetes patula.* a. Detail.
B. French Marigold "Sunny." *Tagetes patula.*
C. Geranium "Red Carefree." *Pelargonium.*
D. African Marigold. *Tagetes erecta.*
E. Cowslip. *Primula veris.*

A.
a.
B.
C.
D.
E.

# *Plate XX*

## *Autumn Flowers • East and West Gardens*

Chrysanthemums. Chrysanthemum and Chrysanthemum *coccineum*

A. "Folksinger."
B. "Headliner."
C. "Kings Ransom."
D. "Lipstick."
E. "Cotswold Gem."
F. "Huntsman."
G. "Scarlet Glow."
H. "Powder River."
J. "Peachstone."
K. "Lemontone."

B.
C.
J.
K.
E.
F.
G.
A.
D.
H.

*Plate XXI*

John F. Kennedy Administration—Spring Flower Arrangement
State Dining Room
Dinner for H.E., The President of The Republic of the Ivory Coast
May 22, 1962

*Vermeil Vase*
Blue Batchelor Buttons
Blue and White Iris
Daisy Type Pompoms
Yellow Chrysanthemums
Yellow Tulips
White Snapdragons
White Pinnochios
Gypsophilia (Baby's Breath)
Podocarpus

## *Plate XXII*

John F. Kennedy Administration
Luncheon for H.E., The President of the Republic of Ecuador
July 23, 1962.

*White Basket*
White Single Chrysanthemums
Blue Hybrid Delphinium
White Majestic Daisies
Blue Globe Thistle
Bermuda Lilies
Red "Happiness" Roses

## *Plate XXIII*

John F. Kennedy Administration
Luncheon for the Foreign Ministers of Latin America
October 2, 1962.
Green Room

*Porcelain Bowl—Chinese Export*
Lowestoft bowls of Yellow Tritoma
Yellow Green Cymbidium Orchids
Yellow Coreopsis
Paperwhite Narcissus
Gaillardia
Yellow and White Marguerite Daisies
Yellow, Orange, Red, and White Zinnias

## *Plate XXIV*

John F. Kennedy Administration—Summer Flower Arrangement
Red Room
Luncheon for President of Cyprus,
His Beatitude Archbishop Makarios III
June 5, 1962

*Tole Monteith Vase*
Red Roses
Rumbrum Lilies
White Pompom Chrysanthemums (Daisy Type)
White Minature Carnations
White Snapdragons
Podocarpus

# *Plate XXV*

## Lyndon B. Johnson Administration—Spring Flower Arrangement
## Green Room

*Chinese Export Porcelain Bowl*
White Delphiniums
Blue Delphiniums
White Miniature Carnations
Marguerite Daisies
White Pompom Chrysanthemums (Daisy Type)
Rumbrum Lilies
Red Chrysanthemums (Daisy Type)
Blue Batchelor Buttons
Podocarpus

# *Plate XXIV*

John F. Kennedy Administration—Summer Flower Arrangement
Red Room
Luncheon for President of Cyprus,
His Beatitude Archbishop Makarios III
June 5, 1962

*Tole Monteith Vase*
Red Roses
Rumbrum Lilies
White Pompom Chrysanthemums (Daisy Type)
White Minature Carnations
White Snapdragons
Podocarpus

# BIBLIOGRAPHY

Aikman, Lonnelle, *The Living White House*, The White House Historical Association and The National Geographic Society, 1970.

*Ballou's Pictorial Companion*

Graff, Paula V., "The Keeper of the President's Trees," *American Forest,* May 1931, p. 288.

*Gleason's Pictorial Drawing Room Companion*

*Harper's Weekly*

Holloway, Laura C., *The Ladies of the White House,* Bradley & Co., Philadelphia, Pa., 1881, p. 735.

Janson, C., *Stranger In America,* 1806, p. 202. (Nicolay Collection—The White House Papers).

Johnston, Frances Benjamin, "The White House," *Demerest's Family Magazine,* May 1890, p. 390.

*Frank Leslie's Illustrated Newspapers.*

Say, Lillian Porter, "Through the White House Fence," *The Christian Science Monitor*, December 19, 1942, p. 14.

Singleton, Esther, *The Story of the White House*, Vol. II. p. 27.

Smith, Philip R., *The Green Acres of The White House*, (unpublished).

Smith, Mrs. Harrison, "The President's House Forty Years Ago," *Godey's Lady's Book,* November 1842, p. 216.

"Strange Features at The White House," *The National Spectator*, April 5, 1926, p. 39.

"Speech of Mr. Ogle," Weeks, Jordan and Company, Boston, Massachusetts, 1840.

Taft, William Howard, "From the White House Windows," *The Breeder's Gazette*, December 18, 1913, p. 1194.

# ACKNOWLEDGEMENTS

*The Publisher wishes to express his deepest appreciation to the following people and institutions whose personal interest and contributions of research material were instrumental in the creation of this book.*

Mr. Clement Conger, Curator, The White House
Mrs. Helen McCain Smith, Press Secretary to Mrs. Nixon, The White House
Mrs. Gwen King, Director of Correspondence for Mrs. Nixon, The White House
Miss Susan Porter, Appointments Secretary to Mrs. Nixon, The White House
Miss Carol Heinsius, Assistant to the Curator, The White House
Mr. Rusty Young, Chief Floral Designer, The White House
Mr. James Nelson, Assistant Chief Floral Designer, The White House
Mr. Irving Williams, Horticulturalist, The White House
Mr. Hillory Tolson, White House Historical Association
Mr. David E. Finley, White House Historical Association
Mr. David Hanna
Mr. Harold T. Pinkett, National Archives
Miss Dorothy Provine, National Archives
Mr. Jerry Kearns, Library of Congress
Mr. John W. Hazard, Kiplinger Washington Collection
Mrs. Gwen Fitzpatrick, Kiplinger Washington Collection
Mrs. Donald Spicer, President General, National Society Daughters of the American Revolution
Daughters of the American Revolution Magazine
Mr. Joshua C. Taylor, Director, National Collection of Fine Arts
Mr. Gene Baro, Director, Corcoran Gallery of Art
Mr. Michael Sterner
Mr. Robert N. Redmond, Gardener, The White House, (July 23, 1923-July 23, 1963)
Mrs. Sonia Wedge, Librarian, The New York Botanical Gardens
Mrs. Lothian Lynas, Librarian, The New York Botanical Gardens

Mrs. Robert A. Lovett
Holland Bulb Company, New York
Mrs. Ray Austrian, The Picture Decorator, Inc., New York
Miss Veronica Geng, Editorial Consultant
Mr. Robert Knudsen, Photographer, The White House
Mr. Dave Powers, John F. Kennedy Library
Mr. Alan Goodrich, John F. Kennedy Library

*THE REPRODUCTION of Harold Sterner's paintings and David Hanna's drawings was supervised by Harvey Hoechstetter of Hoechstetter Printing Company, Pittsburgh, Pennsylvania. All color separation photography was done at Graphic Arts Color Corporation, Pittsburgh, Pennsylvania, entirely from the original art.*

*TYPE FACE used throughout this book is Times New Roman.*

*HOECHSTETTER PRINTING COMPANY printed the book by sheet-fed lithography.*

*THE PAPER is Monadnock Caress, eggshell finish for the text and laid finish Cover for color reproductions.*

*MONADNOCK CARESS is manufactured by Monadnock Paper Mills, Inc., Bennington, New Hampshire.*

*THE COVER FABRIC is Bradford Linen, manufactured by The Columbia Mills, Inc.*

*THE BOOK was bound by A. Horowitz & Son • Bookbinders, Clifton, New Jersey.*

Spring

2. Rose bushes—Nevada. Queen Elizabeth. Pascali. Betty Prior. Kings Ransom. Saratoga. Peace. J. F. Kennedy. 3. Green Pillow Box. 4. Osmanthus. 5. Large English Box. 6. Dusty Miller. 7. Small English Box. 8. Narcissus. Grape Hyacinth. Scilla. Crocus. Fritillaria. 9. Tulips. See East Garden. 10. Catherine Crab Apples.

Summer

11. Columbine. Asters. Petunias. Daisies. Salvia. Delphiniums. Poppys. Yarrow. Plaintain Lilys. Pansies. Nicotiana. Candy Tuft. Primroses. Ladies Mantle. Blanket flower. Peonies.

Autumn

12. Chrysanthemums. Yellow Joanette. Jasmine. Williams. Headliner. Red Mischief. See Autumn planting in East Garden.

**West Garden**

*Planting Layout of North Side.*

*South Side similar.*